THIS BOOK BELONGS TO:

I ♡
MOM

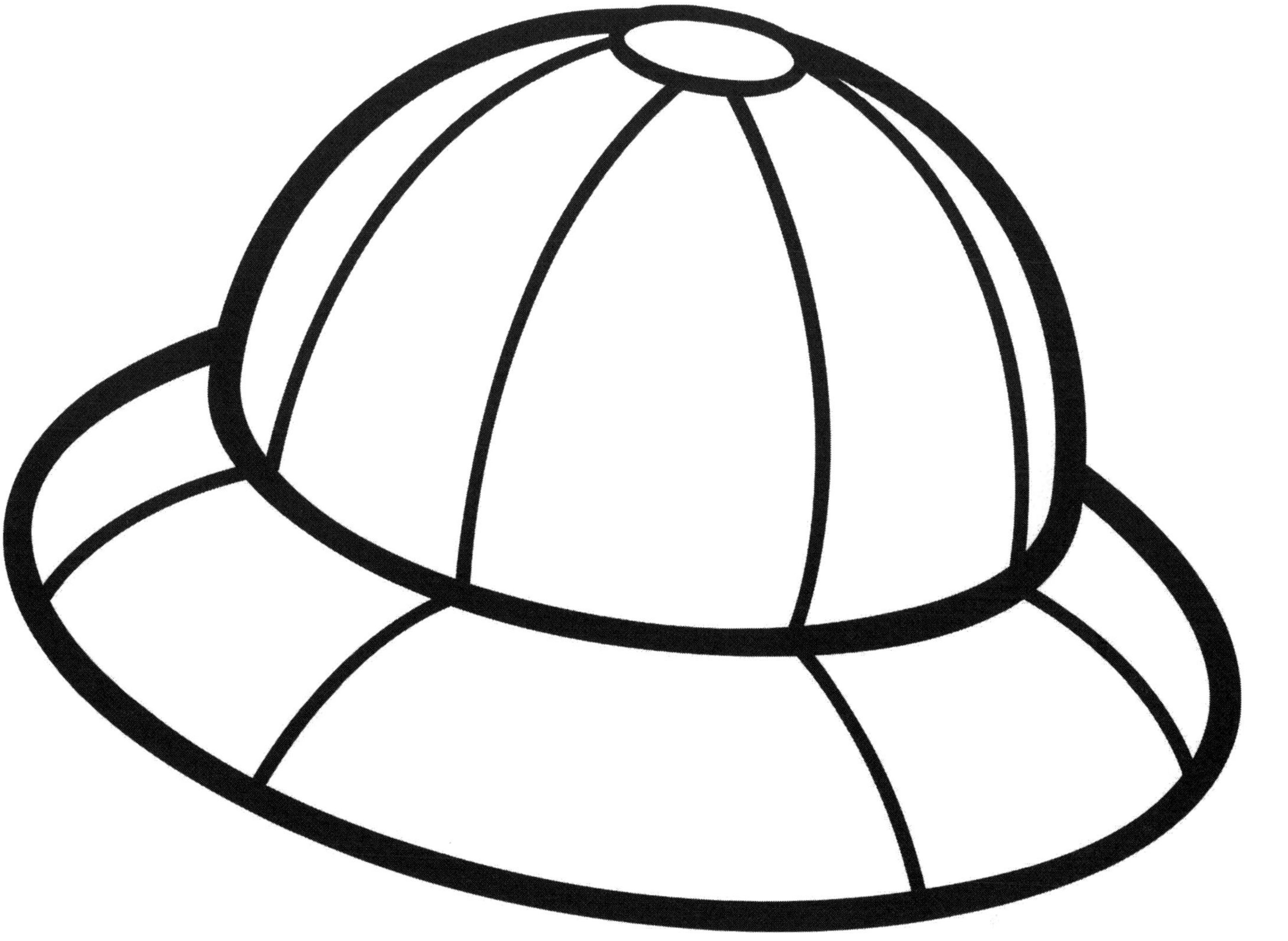

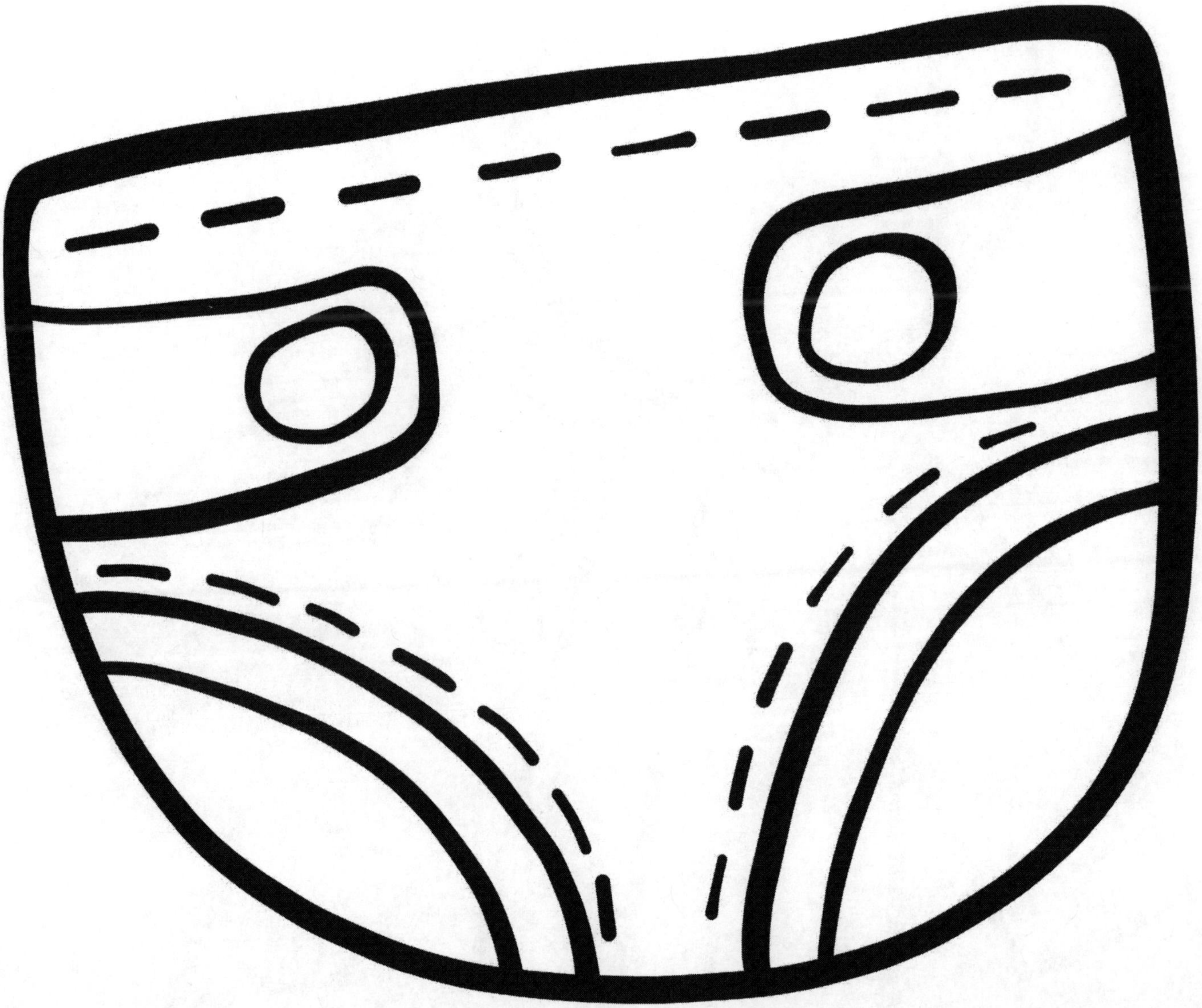

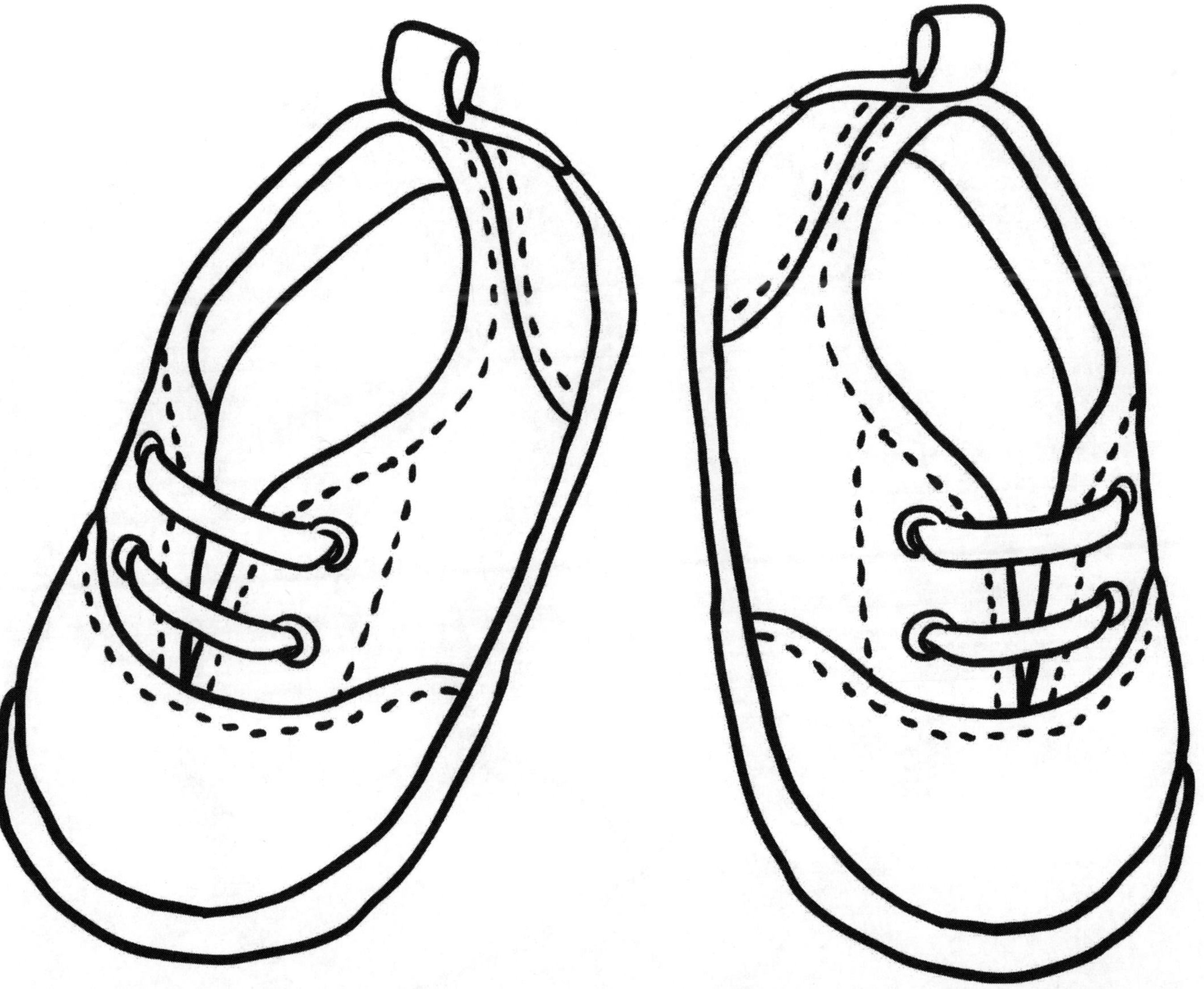

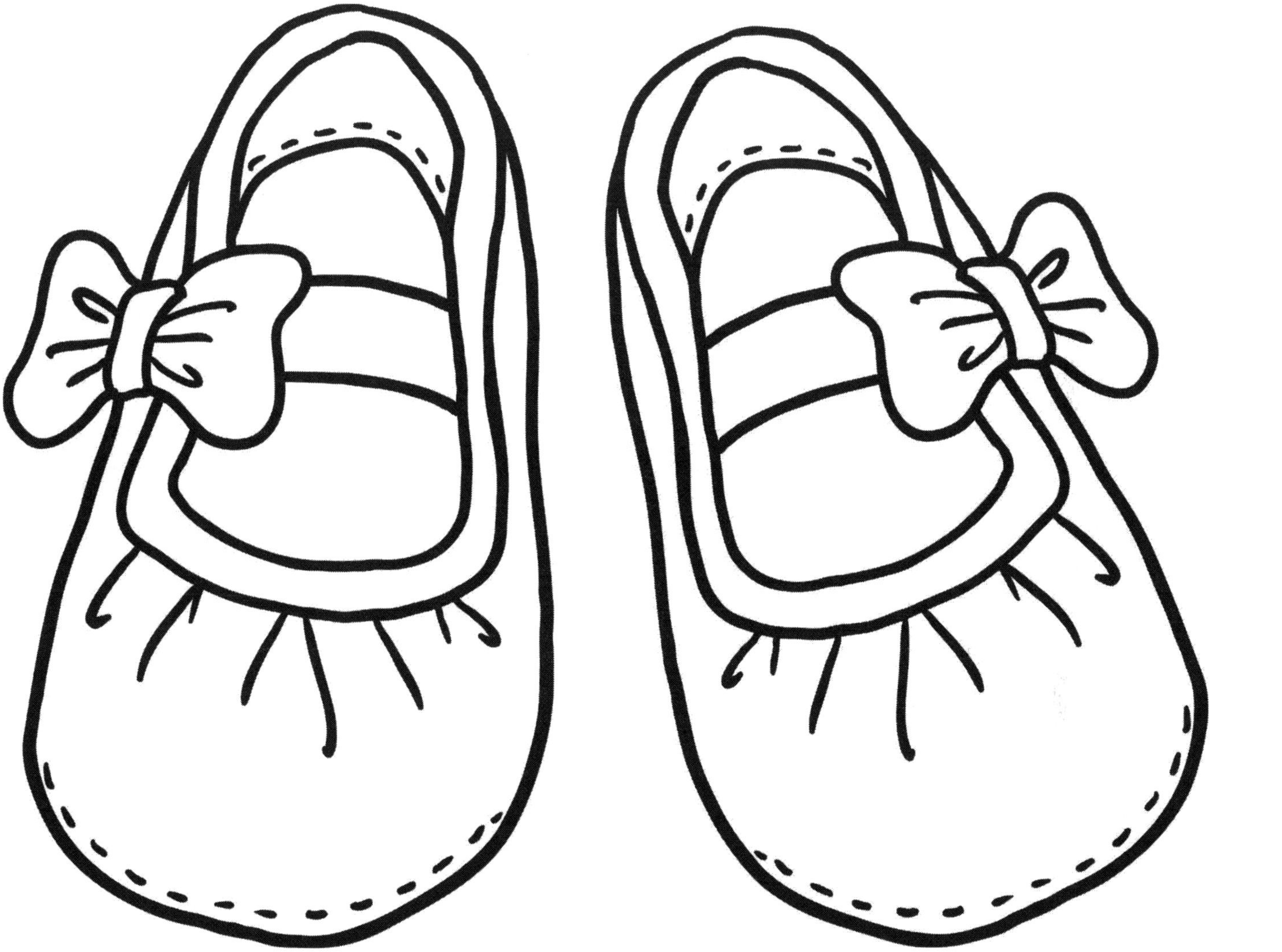

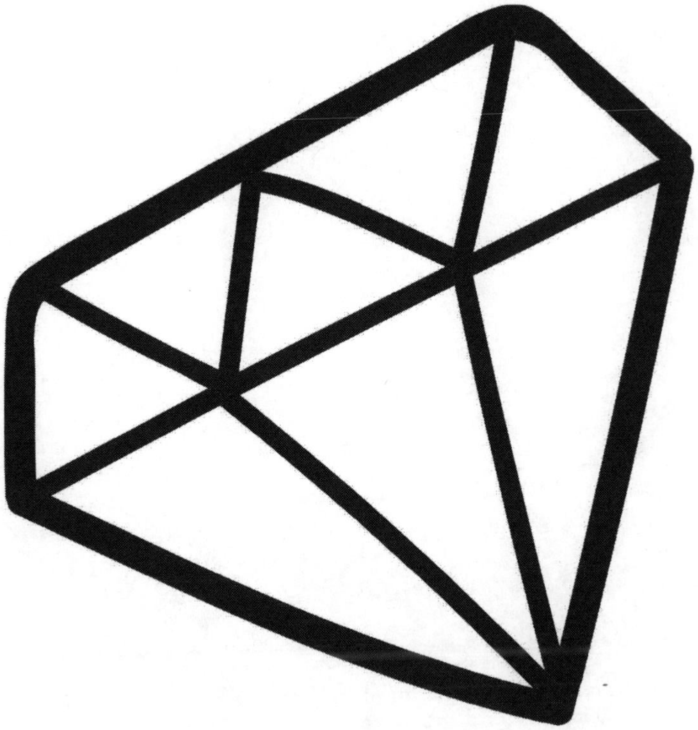

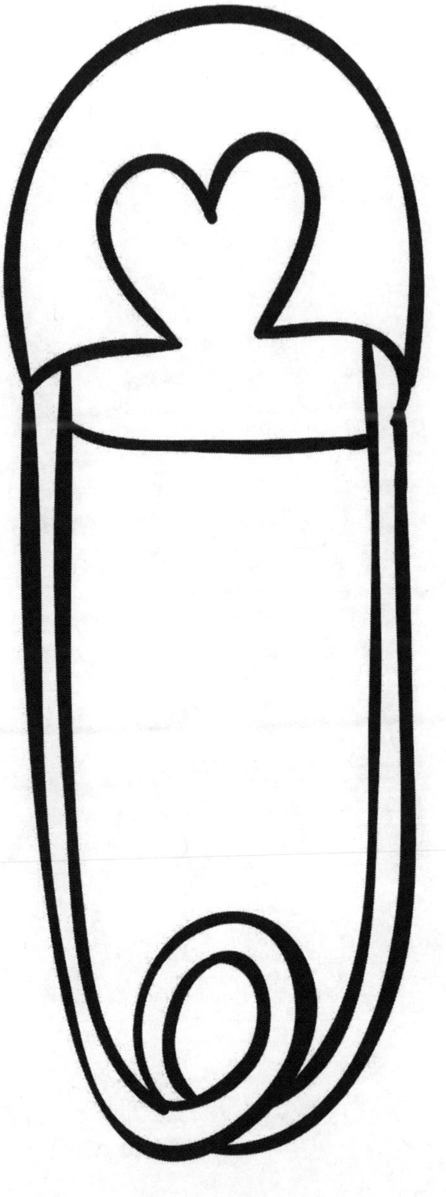

1
2
3

EAST
WEST

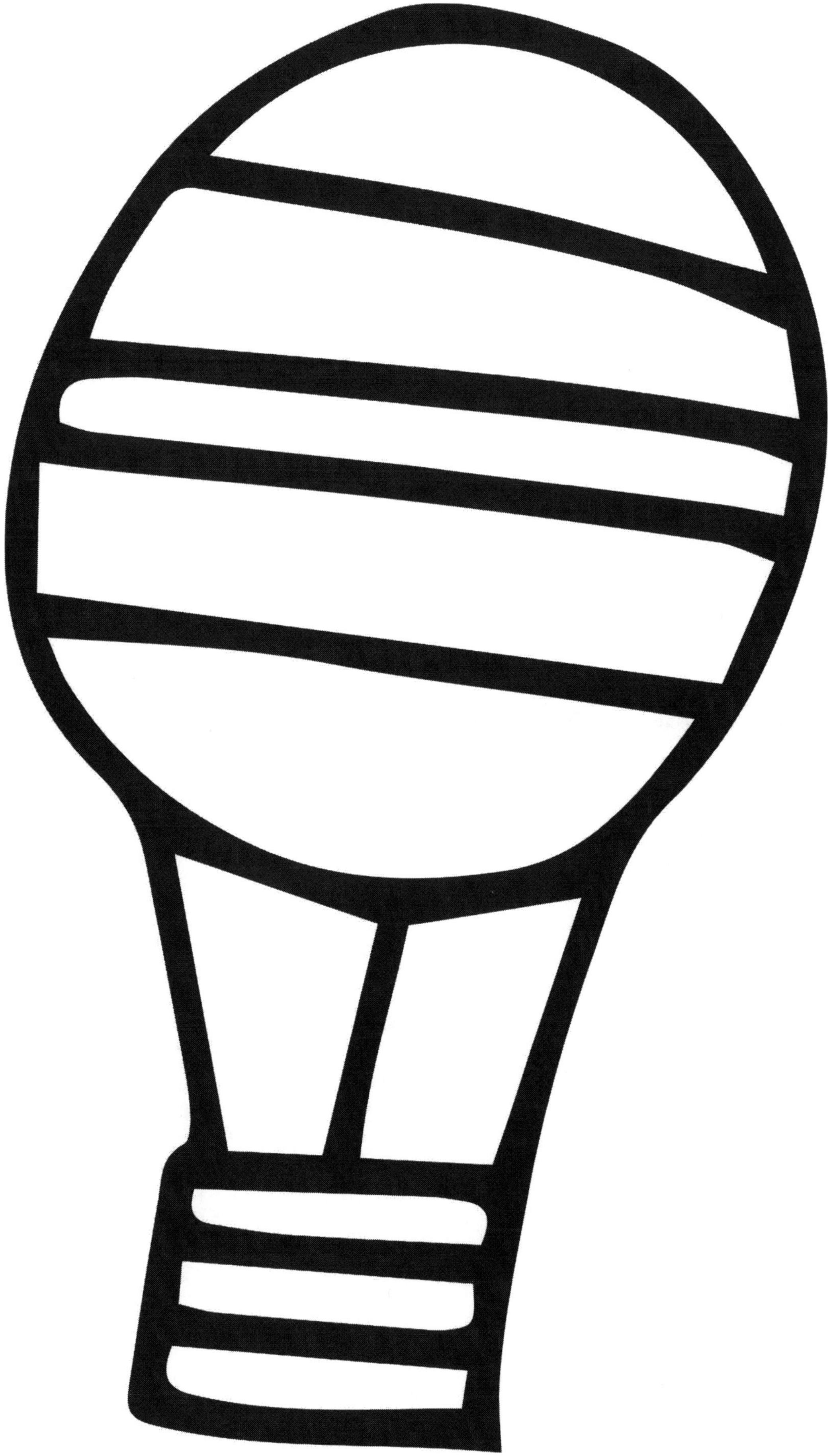

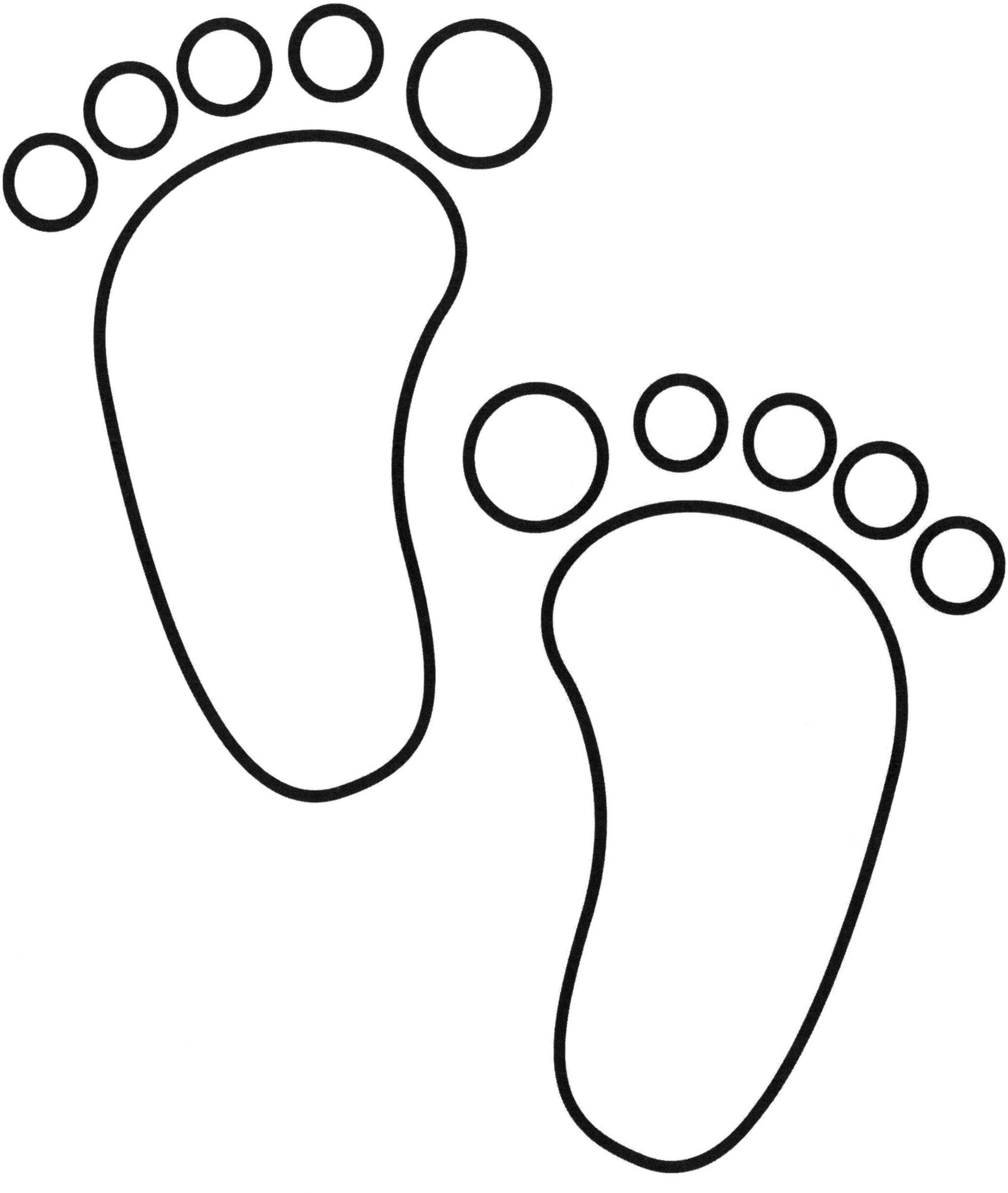

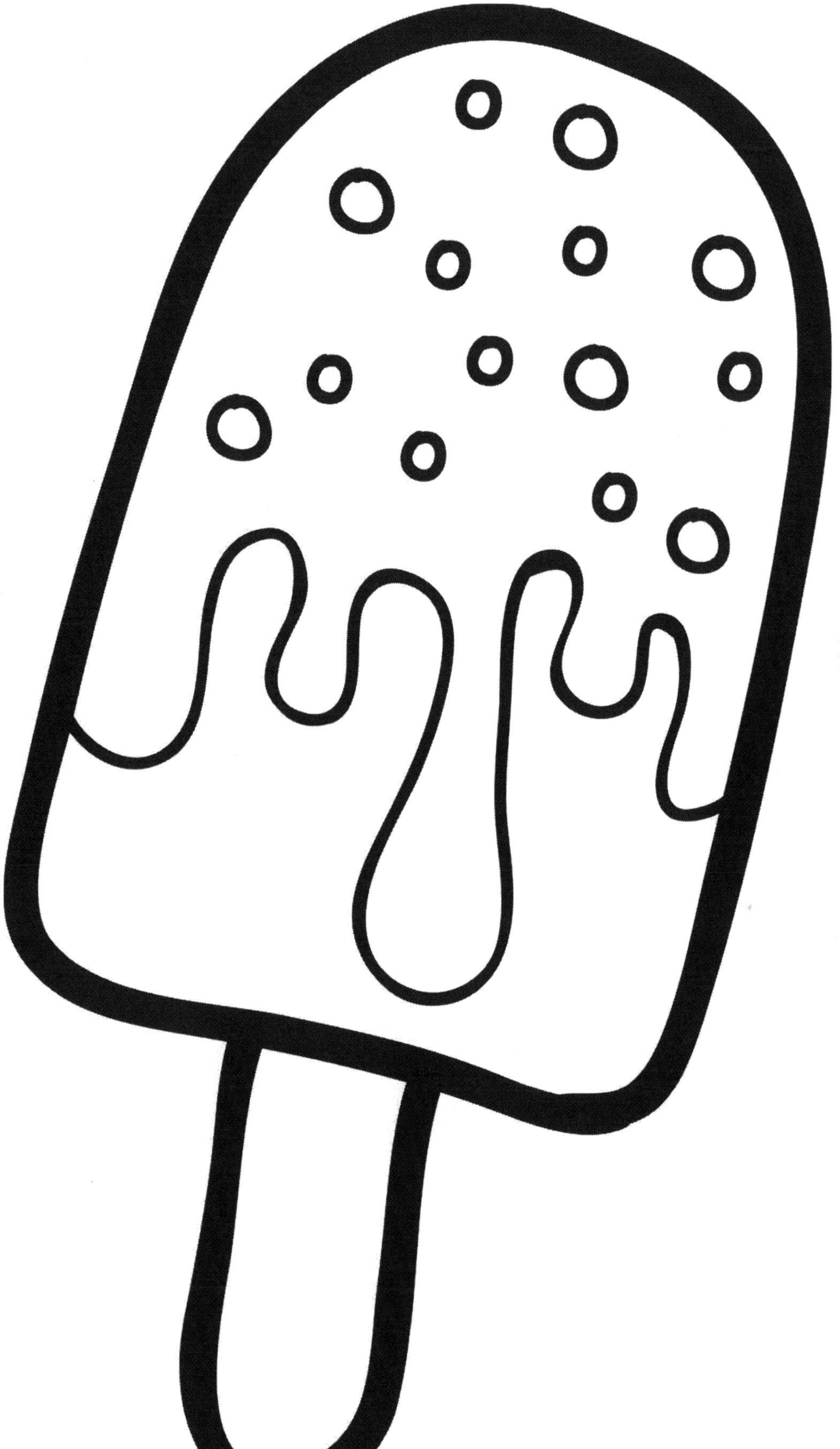

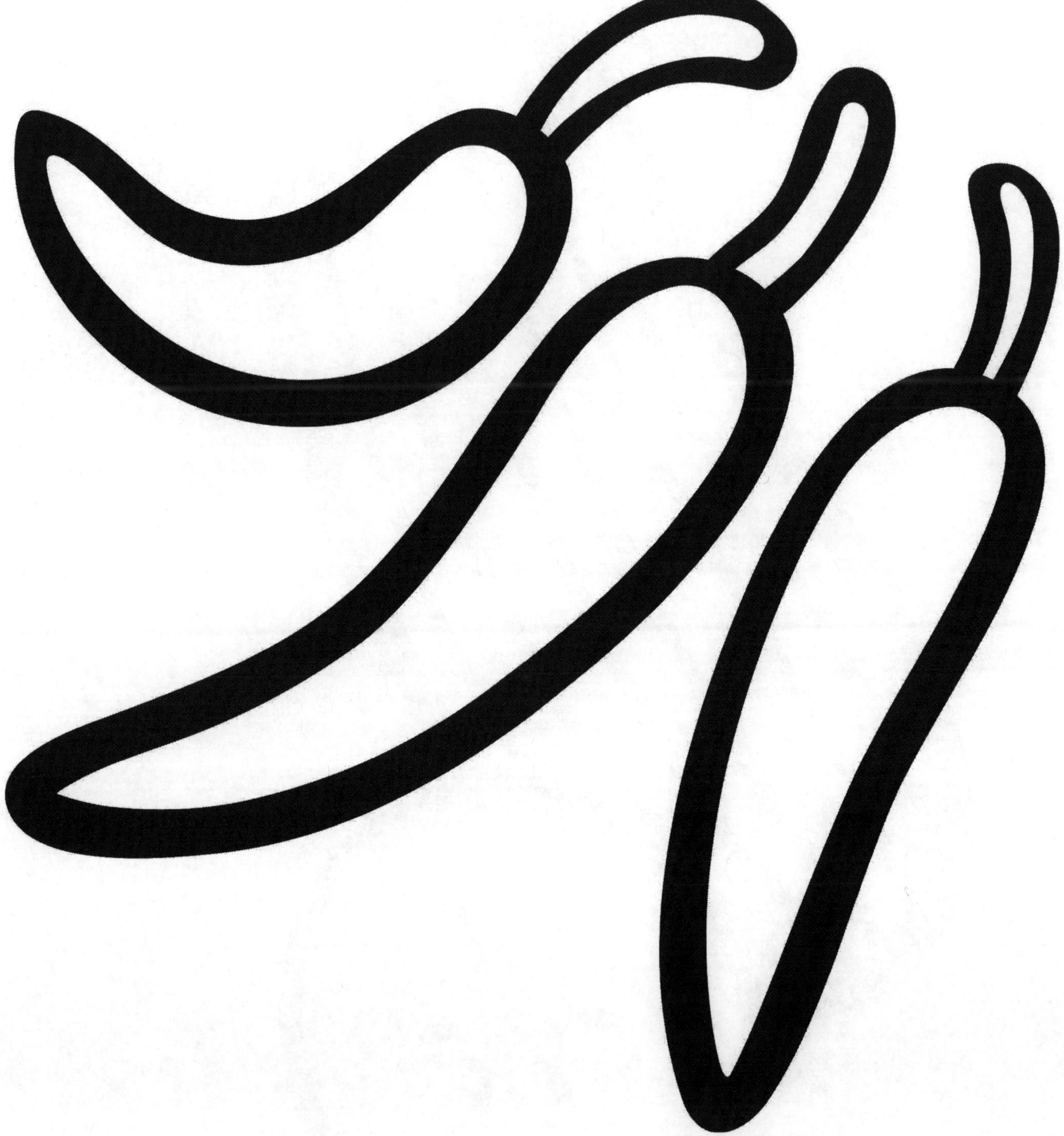

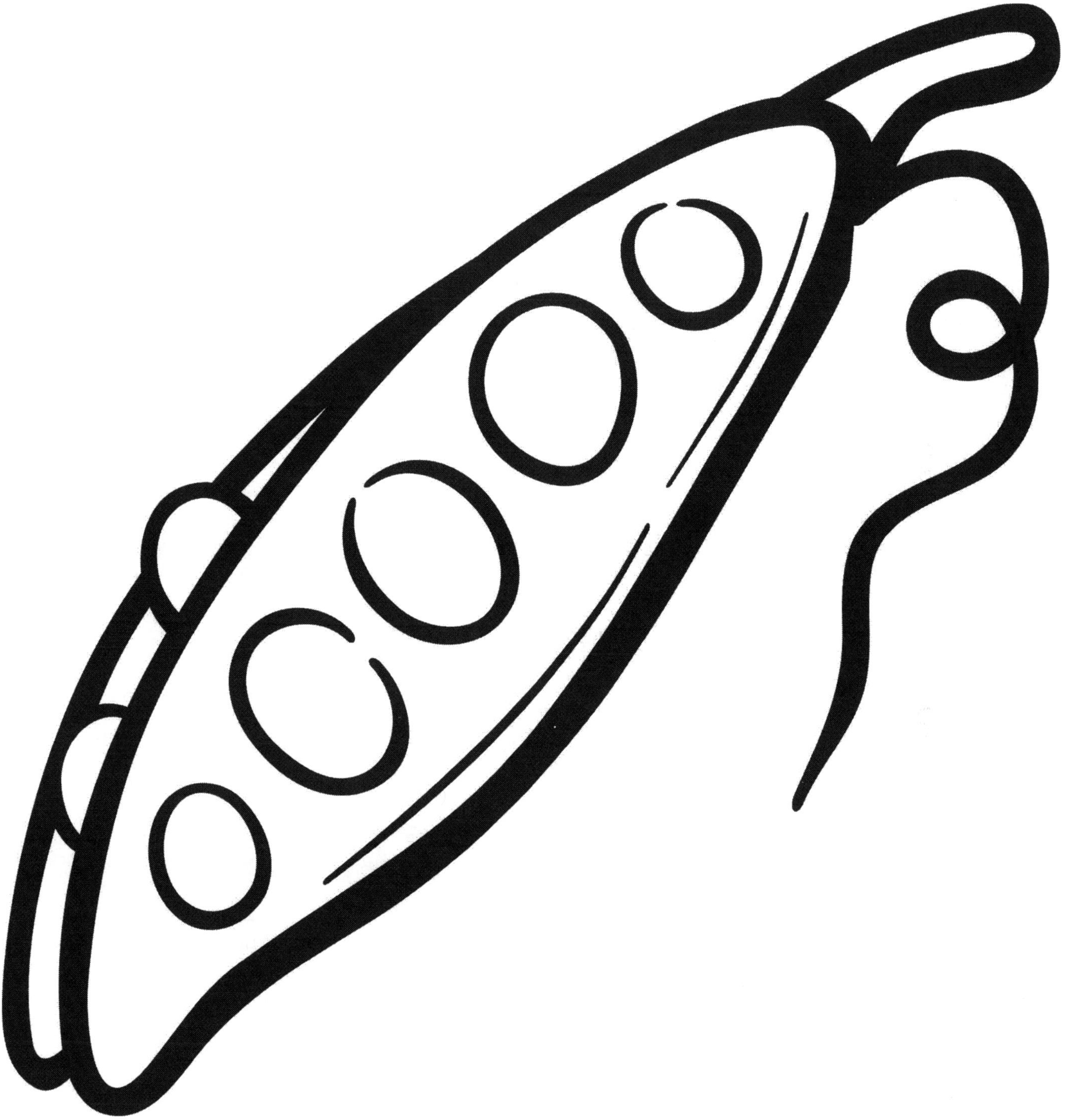

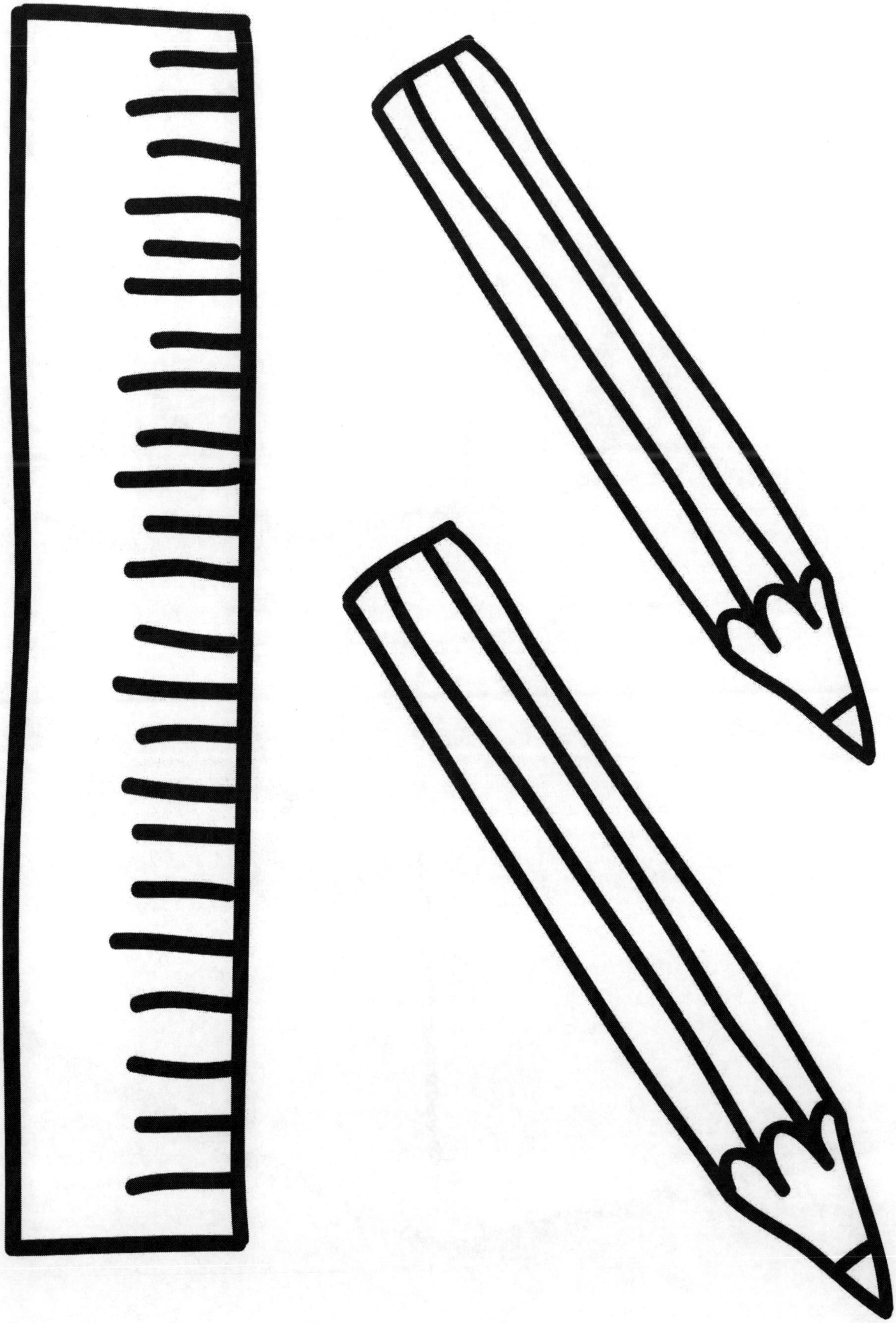

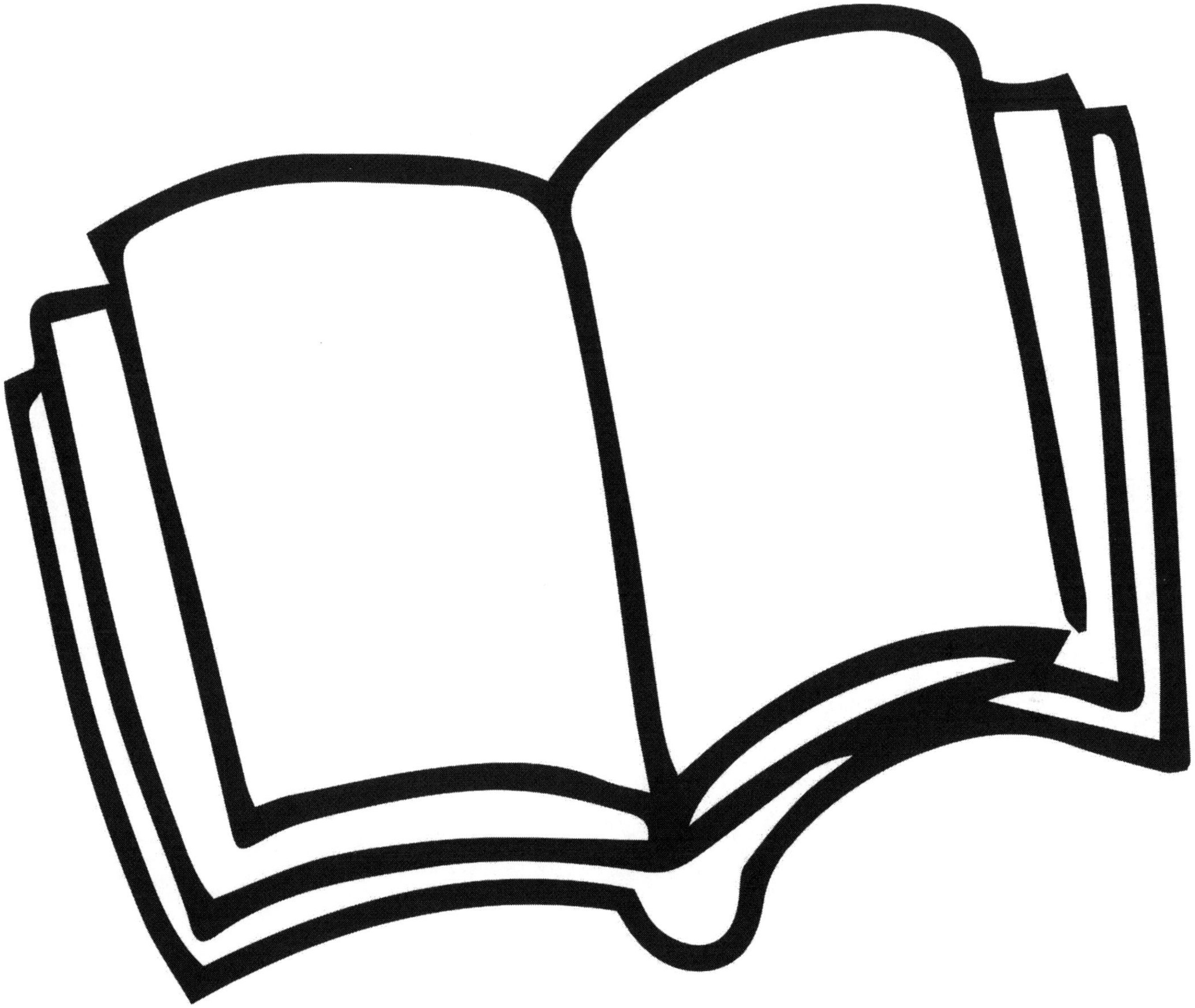

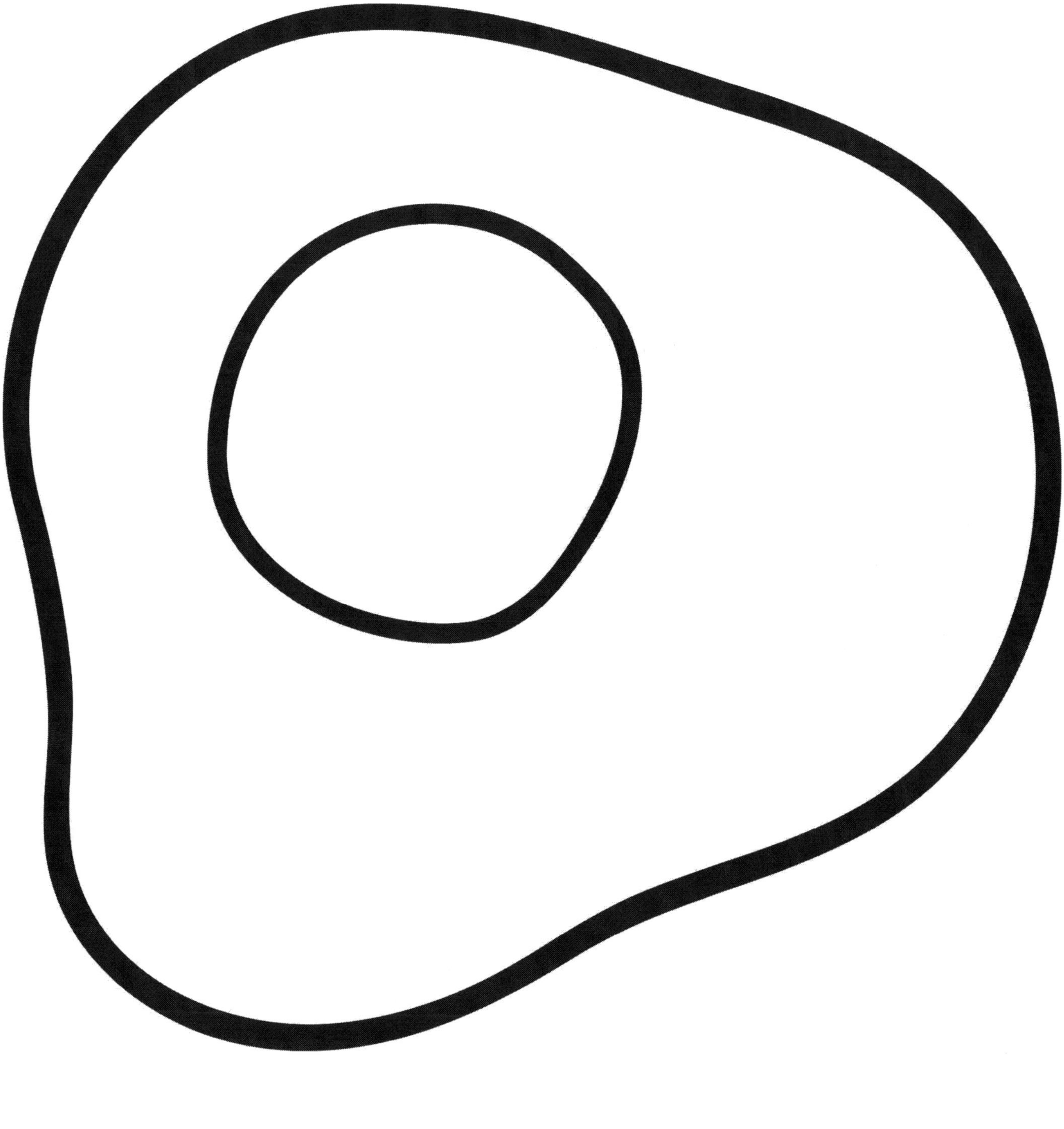

THANK YOU

Made in the USA
Middletown, DE
26 November 2020

25272048R00055